For hearts that are open, revival and renewal in both the personal and corporate realms are about to be birthed through the truths shared in *The Winnowing*.

—Rev. Gloria Willoughby
Manager, Crossroads 24/7 Prayer Centre

From the deep places in her own story, Teena opens up the landscape of suffering as an opportunity and an invitation. If we can turn into the insights she shares with us, rather than run from them, the potential for intimacy with God, deep transformation, freedom and faith will far surpass anything we can comprehend.

—Anna Huws
Ministry Lead, Ffald y Brenin Retreat Centre
and House of Prayer in Wales

The Winnowing is a powerful story of the ever-present faithfulness of God in times of pain and suffering. The author shares her story candidly, inviting the reader to engage with her personal journey through trauma, trouble, and the revelation of the principles and promises in the scriptures that come alive when we go through the crucible experiences of our lives.

As you engage with the author's journey, you will discover many nuggets of truth and wisdom that will edify, encourage, and enhance your faith in God. This story and the lessons learned will confirm unequivocally that God will always be with us and that all things do work together for our good. God will turn the pain and suffering in our lives around for the good.

—Pastors Giulio and Lina Gabeli
Senior Pastors, Westwood Church Network

Embracing the time-honoured legacy of countless saints, Teena's compelling invitation into the intimate realm of her personal journey resonates powerfully, unravelling an intricate tapestry of the meaning of suffering. As we are called to work out our salvation, the presence of "companion guides" often becomes indispensable, rekindling our awareness that God transcends distant skies. He is not far away, but Immanuel—God with us. He is the One well-acquainted with sorrow, who walks with us through our trials and ultimately bears our burdens. Teena's profound insights and transformative odyssey seamlessly join the ranks of these guiding lights, extending a cup of solace to the spiritually thirsty.

—Peter Tufford Kennedy
Writer and performer

Teena has written with vulnerability about her journey through the effects of concussion and loss and finding light at the end of the tunnel. This is a book that will give you hope and the courage to press on to find the treasures of darkness which God has for each of us as we submit to the winnowing.

—Jane Jones
National Prayer Director, Anglican Renewal Ministries
Regional Director, Canadian Firewall

A master class in faith and resilience, this book will renew your spirit. It is a transformative read that shows how to give thanks in all circumstances, making God the One whom we have the most. Brilliantly articulated and soul-stirring.

—Godfrey Adderley
Presbyter, Toronto South, PAOC

I have known Teena for over twenty years and appreciate her openness and authenticity in sharing her journey. We do not discuss suffering openly in Christian circles, yet it is part of everyone's life journey. It's in the seasons of trouble when we are forced to ask tough questions, seek God, and have the potential to grow deeper in our faith and personal relationship with Jesus. When we embrace the challenges, we can move towards the miracles God has for us on the other side. *The Winnowing* is a must read and will change your perspective on suffering!

—Debbie Bolton
Co-founder, Norwex

In *The Winnowing*, Teena Ferrara speaks from a heart of brokenness, sharing her experience with a traumatic brain injury and the tragic death of her twin sister. Hers is a desperate struggle to find peace, comfort, and God in the pain. *The Winnowing* is a triumphant story of waiting, resting, giving thanks, and ultimately healing as God gently takes Teena to the threshing floor of her life, sweeping away the chaff to reveal fine kernels of grain, all for His glory. This book will appeal to anyone who longs to grow in their faith as they, too, face uncertainty and sorrow.

—Barbara Dickson
Author, speaker, and documentary film producer

In *The Winnowing*, the reader will gain a true biblical perspective of what it means to die to self in order that the beautiful new creation of one's heart and soul may emerge from the ashes of life's most difficult human experiences, recognizing that as His children they will be lovingly shaped to be more fully alive to God in refreshingly authentic ways of being!

The subsequent losses as a result of her confinement lead Ferrara on an inner search—one that is not for the faint-hearted but rather for those courageous enough to welcome their Father into the depths of human experience to be with them, and they with Him, in a place of winnowing, where God refines His children for His holy purposes.

Ferrara's discovery of what it means to enter into the fellowship of Christ's sufferings and afflictions (Colossians 1:24) is the countercultural pathway of true discipleship for every pilgrim who are strangers on earth (Hebrews 11:13) following in Jesus's footsteps.

THE
Winnowing

Teena Ferrara

Author photo by Rebekah Mazzacato
www.adorninlightphotography.com

Book cover design & interior illustrations by Cynthia Sayede
cynth.martine@gmail.com

ISBN: 978-1-4866-2498-0
eBook ISBN: 978-1-4866-2499-7

Word Alive Press
119 De Baets Street Winnipeg, MB R2J 3R9
www.wordalivepress.ca

WORD ALIVE
—PRESS—

Cataloguing in Publication information can be obtained from Library and Archives Canada.

This book is dedicated to my loving husband,
Angelo, who saw it all and still loved me.

Acknowledgements

I could not have moved forward in writing this book without the help of Barbara Dickson. You were there at the gate, wading through my messy pages, sharing coffees, and speaking endless encouragement to my heart. Thank you, my friend, for your love and support. Your words were vital to the vision.

Thank you, Cynthia Sayede. Your ability to capture the vision with your original art for these humble pages is stunning. I'm so grateful you said yes.

Julie Wiger, your messages during the darkest, most painful days kept me from giving up. Thank you.

Eileen Simpson, thank you for the mylar balloon. The bobbing happy face was my companion during lonely isolation. Your prayers were my lifeline.

To my children, Sarah (Stephen) and Elisha, thank you for checking in during my confinement and all your love and support along my healing journey.

Finally, I must acknowledge Joan, who suffered in ways I don't understand. Thank you for your joy.

Prelude

In the spring of 2019, I incurred an injury that changed my life. Not everyone is affected the same way that I was. This little book is filled with raw reality and truth. It contains some graphic details about the symptoms I experienced throughout the injury and recovery, and I've tried to describe them accurately. Weaved throughout is my response regarding my faith in God and how He has always led me through, even when I felt completely separated from him.

I've written this book because I felt compelled to share some of the spiritual treasure of knowing God in the midst of our suffering. My prayer is that you will find peace and rest in seemingly unchangeable circumstances in the afflictions of your life. Sometimes hearing other people's stories will encourage you and give you strength to go on when you don't think you can. May you find hope here and, most importantly, the only One that is Hope, Jesus Christ, the soon coming King. He is faithful.

If ye were not Christ's wheat, appointed to be bread in His house, He would not grind you.[1]
—Samuel Rutherford

Beloved, do not be surprised at the fiery trial when it comes upon you to test you, as though something strange were happening to you. But rejoice insofar as you share Christ's sufferings, that you may also rejoice and be glad when his glory is revealed. (1 Peter 4:12–13, ESV)

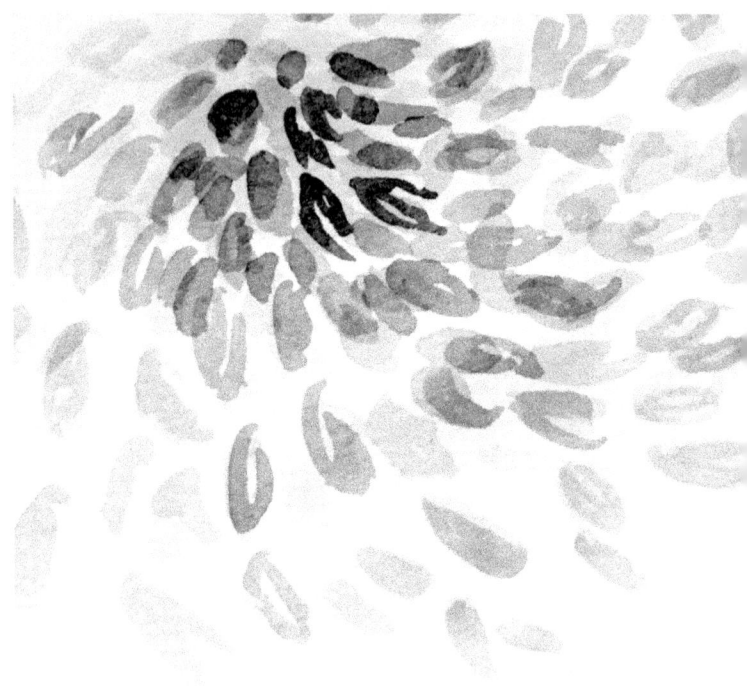

I

Day Ten

This was the day I started to write again. It had been ten days since the injury. I carefully opened a new journal gifted to me by my dear Irish friend and began. I felt wobbly as my eyes followed the curvy ink lines, making ribbons of words on the page. Writing was a challenge and my head was full of blinding pain.

I had to try.

The previous nine days were all I knew. Wild waves had shipwrecked me, violently tossing me side to side and around, thrashing me deep into the sea of confinement, leaving me for dead. I felt buried alive. Underwater. Swimming inside my head in darkness, clothed in separation, clawing the sheets in pain. Sound and light struck at me like a sharpened spear, relentless in their blows and preventing me from walking in the land of the living.

This was day ten. Welcome to my head injury.

The Suddenlies

We often attribute the unexpected happenings of life to either God or the devil. These are the surprises when we suddenly receive a generous gift or promotion. Or some difficult news. It might be an illness, an injury, or the loss of your home, your job, your hope. These unexpected shocks can change everything in a moment. One phone call, one meeting, one encounter, one word. Abrupt and without warning.

It was the first of the month and I was cleaning the house. My energy level was focused and the music kept the beat as I worked. I bent down to pick up something from the floor. All it took was a swift turn to the right...

...and the *suddenly* met the side of my head with the force of a swinging baseball bat, stopping my head, and my body, in its tracks.

Thud.

I felt my teeth grind down hard and I heard myself say, "Ow." There was a split second of my eyes squeezing shut and feeling so very odd. I paused and then shrank to the floor, leaning against the wall in order to get my bearings.

The dog sauntered over and began licking my arm. Dog sense. I did a quick mental body scan. Everything seemed okay.

Standing up, I entered the bathroom and looked in the mirror. Pupils looked fine. No blood anywhere. I checked my tongue for good measure. All seemed well.

The day continued as normal, although I occasionally wondered if there had been any damage.

Nah, I told myself. *I feel fine.*

It wasn't until later in the evening that a new suddenly began to develop and I came to the realization that something was very wrong.

Emergency Room

The emergency room was busy as usual, but with every moment, every second of waiting, my sense of well-being plummeted as panic set in deep and fast.

But finally my husband and I got in to talk with a neurologist behind the curtain divider. Crying and unable to get it together, those blue curtains felt like they were suffocating me. I couldn't breathe and my sense of space was strangely distorted.

"What's going on?" my husband asked me, trying to comfort me, trying to understand what was happening.

"Angelo, I miss my sister…" I loud-whispered, my voice shaky and unstable. "I don't want to be in the hospital…"

My body trembled from head to toe and all I wanted to do was crawl out of my skin, out of my skull.

The doctor completed her exam and confirmed that I had a TBI, a traumatic brain injury, also known as a concussion. After the CT scan, we were sent home with nothing but a directive to see our family doctor as soon as possible. The end. There was little discussion or instruction—just the recommendation to take the maximum Tylenol dose for pain and an offer to be prescribed anti-anxiety meds.

I was confused. We didn't know anything about concussions. Even so, what I was about to experience can hardly be described in words.

This was night one, the beginning of my journey into the belly of the whale.

Lent

We were in the middle of the Lenten season, one of my most favourite seasons on the Christian calendar. I was observing this sacred time with various scripture readings and prayer, following them along with rich devotions by Henri Nouwen. I also had a heightened focus on my heart's true condition.

A few weeks earlier, I'd visited a traditional church on Ash Wednesday. The historical building had been dimly lit and unlike the vibrant faith community we partnered with.

I reverently made my way down the long centre aisle. The sound of my shoes bounced around the room, echoing throughout the massive space as I tried not to let my heels touch the floor, tiptoeing and looking very awkward.

I sat with a handful of other parishioners on the hard, worn oak benches. They quietly greeted me with smiles and nods.

The mood was sombre and hushed, and I wasn't sure what I was doing there. I looked down at the floor while the minister spoke.

Tears snuck out of my eyes like greased marbles and dropped onto my lap, marking my jeans. It had only been seven weeks since my twin sister, Marni, had unexpectedly died. My chest burned with pent-up sorrow. Like a dog waiting by the door to be let out, my grief was uncontainable. Trying was futile.

When it was time, I stepped forward with the others. The minister came close and made the sign of the cross on my forehead with his thumb trailing thick black ash.

"Remember that you are dust, and to dust you shall return," he intoned.

Yes, we are all dust, and we will all return to dust. A stark reminder that life is fragile.

I walked outside onto the busy sidewalk, marked with the smudge of Ash Wednesday for all to see. I zipped up my coat, got into my car, and drove home.

The Lenten season is the heart of Christianity; Christ has died, Christ has risen, Christ will come again. It's the journey into Easter weekend, reminding us as we ponder the death and resurrection of Christ that He loved us first, that death is imminent and resurrection life a free gift. It's a most spiritually deepening season for all who follow Jesus of Nazareth and his ways, for all who have found forgiveness.

This season, I had a specific prayer focus: "Father, please give me the heart that I do not have, the one that I want, a heart that is never offended."

This was a big ask, but a needful one in order to grow more spiritually mature. I was weighing my true condition as I offered my all to the Lord. It seemed out of reach to harbour no offence at all, but this ideal clearly reflected the character of Christ. We are to prevent offence from entering our hearts and having dominion over us.

I knew I was unable to change my own heart. My attempts to do so always ended the same. It would take a work of the Holy Spirit to bring me to that place. My heart already wasn't easily offended, but I wanted to go further; I wanted absolute, ongoing freedom.

But now the effects of my head injury weighed heavily on me, pressing in and walling me in. At this juncture, it was impossible to reconnect with my steps on the Lenten pathway. My unexpected trajectory into solitude and helplessness left me in an ongoing state of surrender and weakness, unable to control the symptoms that dictated my days and nights.

Yes, this was to be a very different season of Lent. What an intense trial I suddenly found myself in! The dark night of the soul was upon me, but God chooses ways we would never choose. His ways are so much higher than ours.

Trauma

> As for me, I said in my haste and alarm, I am cut off from before Your eyes. But You heard the voice of my supplications when I cried to You for aid. (Psalm 31:22)

Days into the head injury, I am spending most of my time on either the living room couch or my bed, regularly dosing myself with pain medication and trying to sleep. Earplugs and eye covers dull my senses and keep me hidden from the world.

My pace is turtle slow. I have to hold the wall to climb the stairs, taking one step at a time. Every movement feels like lifting a body full of broken bones.

I seem unable to hoist myself out of this womb of suffering, with each day bringing new symptoms.

After spending a few minutes outside on the front porch, I head straight back into the house and settle onto the couch, overwhelmed by the light, sound, and movement of the world. I have no filters against it. Raw reality.

The perpetual panic feels like a real-time horror show. As if tripping on a bad street drug, I start to experience borderline hallucinations. Is some stranger standing beside my bed? I can hear them breathing and moving! How will I get up and run downstairs? I am all alone and the pain in my head is unbearable. I can't pray. I can't remember any scriptures or worship songs. All I have are incomplete fragments: "Our Father in heaven…" and "The Lord is my Shepherd…"

My mind races, searching for something to draw from the internal well, hewn and filled from years of following Jesus, the Word hidden in my heart. Where is it? Why can't I access it? I can't think, can't remember anything. I am panicking in the dark, my ears ringing so loudly that it hurts. I feel weak all over, and the pain in my head is like shrapnel going off. It scares the heck out of me.

I can't control this. I'm going out of my mind, fear swallowing me up. All I can do is weep amidst this waking torment.

I get up and try to get down the stairs as quickly as possible, not sure if anything of this is real. Maybe it's a nightmare?

When I pass the mirror, I catch a glimpse of myself and see a frightening image. I find the couch and break down.

"Jesus, where are You?" I cry out in a weak voice. "I can't see You here! Where are You? Show me where You are!"

I wait in the grip of this ethereal state, feeling separated from God. This feeds into my actively anxious thoughts. I have gone through ten days of this!

Another wave of fear clutches at my breathing. The relentless panic attacks seem to have no end. Day after day, night after night, the pattern repeats. I can't believe this is happening.

Doctors Appointment

Sunglasses on, earplugs in, and relying on my husband's steady arm, I got into the car for the white-knuckled drive to my doctor's appointment. I couldn't look out the window because the movement of the cars induced fresh lashes of seasickness and had me rolling in my perception of space.

When we finally arrived, I sat quietly in the dimmed office, the sunglasses shielding me. She spoke kindly, offering me options to manage my symptoms. But she knew something I still didn't: that this was going to be a very long road, head injuries are a tricky beast and recovery requires much prayer and endurance.

"What you need right now is patience," she stated matter-of-factly from across her desk. "You need lots of time. It could take six months, maybe even a year, before you're better."

My expression must have set off alarm bells in her, because she leaned back in her chair.

"Why do you think athletes take a year off?" she went on, driving home her point. "They're motivated by millions of dollars, but they still take the time they need. A year or more. They can't play with this type of injury."

Her words hung heavy. My wobbly brain tried very hard to process what she was saying. In disbelief, I rejected these words with all I could muster. What on earth was she saying? Six months? A year even? I was in shock, attempting to grasp that this wouldn't go away in a week or two.

My active life had just come to a complete halt.

I asked about the off-the-charts fear and panic and indescribable head pain.

"Doing things isn't hurting your brain," she told me. "But the pain you experience reinforces your fears."

Somehow this was a relief—to understand that my attempts at simple tasks, like taking a shower, weren't worsening my injury even though it felt like it.

If I thought about this statement more deeply, that the pain I experience reinforces my fears, it spoke to something else within me. It confronted my hidden fear of abandonment. My past negative experience re-inforced the fear of it happening repeatedly.

As with my body's kneejerk responses now, I would cover my noggin when I heard a loud noise or saw something near my head. This is my injury memory. We conclude that past experience predicts future experience, expecting the same patterns to repeat.

For me, the pattern included my fear of abandonment due to my twin sister's death, of being left behind, excluded, and rejected. Losing her so unexpectedly had sparked a fear of being alone. It created in me a temporary sense of being abandoned by my sister. But my doctor's words did offer some comfort.

I hadn't expected this. Could she have presented an instant remedy? A three-step cure?

After scheduling my next appointment, this time for the neurology and concussion clinic, we drove home and I carefully got out of the car. It had been a big day and I just wanted to die.

Neurologist

Finally, with anticipation, we made our way to the concussion clinic. The rush hour drive kept me hostage in the passenger seat. I told myself this was a good thing and would help me get better.

We carefully entered the building from the sidewalk and walked into a bright open space. We took a seat… and I immediately entered the red zone. Why was it so bright in here? Why was it so noisy? This was a TBI clinic, so why was it like this?

Three… two… one… meltdown. Panic broke out and I felt totally overwhelmed. It seemed like we were kept waiting forever.

At last we were invited into a tiny office space where one of the therapists spoke to us. She saw my instability and suggested that we could rebook for another time if I wasn't up to continuing.

But I decided to push myself. There were a lot of questions that needed answering, and we took our time, taking multiple five-minute breaks along the way to get through. I don't remember anything we talked about. I don't remember whether we saw any other doctors. And I certainly don't remember booking another appointment.

Once we got home later that day, I wrapped myself up on the couch in the hope of finding respite. The soft flannel blanket soothed me as I burrowed down, flooded with intense migraines.

Community

Spaghetti Tuesdays! We ate, shared, and prayed together at our biweekly house group, filling our home with love and laughter. It was a beautiful gathering of sons and daughters, hungry hearts, stumblers, and overcomers.

The table had become an important element of our spiritual lives. I enjoy preparing and serving meals. For us, it was about Christ with us, desiring to be welcomed by us again during our communion together as one body. The delight this brings our Father, who loves to see and hear us in a place of unity and love, is palpable. He designed us for friendship and love.

Missing these meetings was a heartbreak. Knowing I was quietly resting in the bedroom upstairs as they gathered in the dining room below me was a great source of pain. I could hear forks clanging on plates and the sweet sound of fellowship.

If only I could find rest here in the shallow waters of despair.

Oh how I longed for my faith community, my family and friends. I craved human contact, drinking frothy chai tea and lattes in oversized mugs, snacking on sweet and savoury treats, snuggling up on the porch with glowing candles. Offering spontaneous prayer, a hallelujah, a hug. I so missed the deep kinship that quickens in every believer when we gather. In such a place our needs can be heard, our hearts cheered, and our thanksgiving shared.

Allowing others to see our inner selves means allowing others to see Christ in us, the living God. Withholding ourselves from others is akin to withholding Christ. When I withhold my friendship from others, I also withhold the friendship of Christ.

This is the fascinating mystery of the body of Christ. He is the head; we are the body, his arms and legs on the earth, ransomed by the blood of the Lamb, his holiness pumping through our veins. We are a physical representation of Him for all to see. Even as we forgive and love one another, every part of this body must remain connected, every muscle and sinew tied together for eternity, both here and on the other side in the age to come. This is our forever family.

In the lonely days of recovery, as I curled up in a ball on the couch, I stared at a mylar balloon with a sunny face bobbing in the corner. It was a get-well delivery from my friend. I then shifted my gaze towards the dark wooden dining table across the room and lamented to God, "Lord, I just want to serve! I just want to serve those around our table."

Right then, the Lord spoke with a swift word to my heart. Immediately I was impressed with the image of two sisters: Mary and Martha. Martha, who was occupied serving people, and Mary, who had learned to sit and wait at Jesus's feet. I also saw that Jesus wasn't going to agree with Martha's demand to make Mary change her posture in order to help with dinner. The better thing was Mary's great act of being still.

In my journal, I wrote these words: "Don't underestimate this. Be still, wait, and rest; listen to him." In that moment, I understood Christ's words: *"Mary has chosen the better portion… which shall not be taken away from her"* (Luke 10:42).

There it was. Learn to be still, to wait and listen. Do not neglect the waiting and the stillness. When I doubted whether I'd ever return to community, this perspective came with a sigh. This whole nasty experience was leading me into a chilling and beautiful place of solitude.

The great wait was upon me.

Brain

It's difficult to understand the effect that sounds have on a healing brain. Tapping laptop keys, a light switch, a door closing, footsteps… any of these would hurl me into a torrent of tears and anger. Light in every spectrum was pain-inducing.

A couple of months post-concussion, I was finally able to listen to a complete song with only a medium amount of wincing.

What do you do when you're locked up in sensory prison and there's no music to soothe your soul? No humming, no birdsong, no rest granted from an instrument of praise. I couldn't even tolerate my own voice. I couldn't engage in conversations with anyone other than my husband and children. My halted speech and broken sentences were exhausting. If anything, the absence of sound brought relief.

This unpleasantness caused me to reach out to God, the One who was able to meet me in my weakness, my brokenness. Yet in that empty place, it seemed as though I was to continue on in despair, trapped in a state of separation and confinement far beyond my expectations. The sorrow from my sister's death was still like a black sea sloshing around the rim of my heart, continually overflowing, a constant reminder that she was gone. I no longer had the capacity to manage this loss.

My day-to-day existence was framed by something called "active rehab." I'm thankful for these new findings in medicine, but I had work to do in my recovery. If I wanted results, it would have to come incrementally. At first I would be able to walk out the front door, and eventually find my way around the block. It sounds silly, but the reality is that the thought of going for a walk brought on a plethora of symptoms from high anxiety to fierce meltdowns. When these symptoms arose, I was instructed to stop immediately and go back inside to the safe wrappings of my quiet cocoon.

But each day I had to walk a wee bit further. And each day I retreated to the cocoon.

It took many weeks before I was able to walk around the block without experiencing the dreaded red zone.

That's just how it goes with head injuries. The brain is an interesting heap of grey matter. Quite magnificently made are we. Miraculous beings made from love!

Our creator uses seasons like these to allow us to see different parts of himself, parts we might not otherwise learn about. Selah.

When the emotional component of my injury arose, it was deep and moving and full, as if I were consumed by a vast, crashing tidal wave. It weaved in and out of my days and wakeful nights in crests of great emotional pain. I needed to hear the sound of strings and keys and the hush of voices in grateful worship to the King of Glory. I could only listen for a second, as the sounds would trigger sensations that reminded me of electrocution. My brain was still unable to filter music, leaving me in my chamber of deafening trauma, helpless and confined, very aware of the veil behind which I was hidden.

Suffering affects the mind. Some of our thoughts can be very negative, leading to depression and hopelessness. These unwelcome thought processes flicker within us and keep us in a place of bondage and unrest. Through the journey of healing, however, the mind begins to return to its right order in areas that may have been messy before. Our negative thoughts can be stilled as we renew our minds. This is a lifelong process of learning and discipline as followers of Christ.

Our busy, preoccupied lives can manifest negativity, including restlessness, lack of sleep, and uncontrolled thoughts. The solution is the discipline of continually returning to a place of still water. Our minds are renewed by being washed in the words of

God, the scriptures, and the revealing of Christ. We eat of the living bread and drink of the cup in sweet communion with Christ and others. In humility, we surrender and turn our trust over to the Father.

God had created my brain and knew everything about my situation. Right there, right where I was—even right where you are—God sees and hears us.

> …who by [the help of] faith subdued kingdoms, administered justice, obtained promised blessings, closed the mouths of lions, extinguished the power of raging fire, escaped the devourings of the sword, out of frailty and weakness won strength and became stalwart, even mighty and resistless in battle, routing alien hosts. (Hebrews 11:33–34)

Was it possible that by faith I could be made strong, mighty, and unbeatable in battle? Could I put enemy forces to flight while still in my weakness?

The letter to the Hebrews gives us a list of what men and women of faith were capable of. They accomplished so much by faith. It's about our faith in Christ Jesus. Our faith is at the root of our battles.

Birthday

Today is my birthday. *Our* birthday. It's four months since my twin died and six weeks since my concussion.

I'm a mess, sobbing and full of pain in my heart and head. I feel the twist of separation, both in the land of the living and my cerebral perception, the result of broken neurons.

I relive the final night with her in the hospital and feel all over again the unanswered questions, the shocking image of seeing her in the empty hallway, blanketed on the gurney as the nurses whisked her from surgery to the ICU right before my eyes. They stopped multiple times to make adjustments, their worried expressions unlatching my guarded demeanour.

I can hear myself yell after her in the late hours of the night, "I love you, womb mate! I love you, twinny!" I sobbed in my husband's arms, having collapsed to the floor of the waiting room, wrecked on impact.

Snapping out of the flashback, I sit up on the couch in my drowning remembrance and ask the Lord to send someone. I've had only meagre outside human contact for the last six weeks, but suddenly I need a familiar face.

In just a few minutes, in the midst of the storm, I hear the ring of the doorbell. Two church friends, armed with fresh tulips and a hug, step inside right on time. I don't make any sense as I ooze out blathering words that sound like "I'm so glad you're here… I just prayed for someone to come… The florist got my order wrong… Oh my gosh, sorry, I'm such a mess but the order was wrong… How could they get it wrong…?"

Amidst even more emoting, more blurting, I awkwardly try to contain this oil spill of a verbal disaster. I'm embarrassed, but their kindness and grace are so authentic. While thoughts bombard me, I tell myself to relax… just relax…

But I care about what they see and what they've just walked into. Well, it's too late. This unravelling is far from over.

Pain

Where does it hurt?
You dig around my heart like a dog in the dirt
All that soil, falling like oil
Through your holy hands
Where does it land? You watch over it all
And sometimes I complain about it, try to sustain my
comfort, to refuse to suffer,
Only to find, I'll never know you as my healer, the
sealer of my heart.
Pain
Some say without it there is no gain
But I can see that in your blood stain, on my soul,
marked there,
It's your name... ingrained upon my heart, pierced
and in your palm of your hand,
Written in your book of life, eternal
My gain, it's in the truth that invades the heart like
healing balm
The trusted One who liberates me into the main
thing, the only thing
Sustaining me in the out-raying of your glory
Where I find you, warm and kind
Pain
Forging me in the wilderness,
The desert hot and dry
A flame, a cry, eternal treasures etched in soul
Waking me, drawing me
Enabling the weak knees and hanging arms,
Up and over the hills, leaning on my Beloved.

I have been crucified with Christ. It is no longer I who live, but Christ who lives in me. And the life I now live in the flesh I live by faith in the Son of God, who loved me and gave himself for me. (Galatians 2:20, ESV)

II

Winnowing

I had so many unanswered questions. What was God saying to me in all this? Why did I think this had happened? From the early days of the concussion, I remember thinking about how important it was for me to interpret what had happened rightly. God abided in me and his presence was with me. How it had happened wasn't really important, but it was of the utmost importance to perceive where I was now.

I had no way to engage in practical spiritual warfare, other than to cry out to God in my darkest confinement. Some people told me it was an attack of the devil. Others just assumed I must have a secret sin.

Scripture teaches us to give thanks *in* all circumstances, not *for* all circumstances. That bit of instruction is intended for our good. So how was I to interpret this whole situation? I called out for God to resurrect me out of my broken bed of pain.

And in due time, He did raise me up again.

As I thought about everything that had happened, this is what I understood: the Lord wasn't punishing me. This situation wasn't the result of some sin, and it wasn't a targeted attack of the devil. God wasn't upset with me or ignoring me. He was speaking to me. Even while pleading to escape, I had to come to a place of surrender where I was free to let things be. I had to "just accept it," as my doctor would say.

But what if this was an arrow of the enemy of my soul? What if the Lord had allowed me to be harmed? Had Job given attention to the devil when he lost everything, including the sudden death of his family?

This really was a threshing floor, where harvesters go to winnow their grain. The wind catches the outer shell of the grain that's been crushed and beaten, whisking away the unusable bits and discarding them across the land. This same winnowing occurs in my life and yours. God's purposes in this are clearly taught throughout the scriptures, which use language like *refiner's fire*, *fuller's soap*, *tempests*, *storms*, *tribulations*, *sufferings*, and *sifting*.

In the natural, the winnowing process involves heavy labour. During the harvest, the stalks of grain must be cut down and laid out to dry. Then it is beaten out with rods and stomping feet in order to loosen the kernels. This is typically done at the threshing floor. The broken grain is then tossed into the air to be blown away by the wind. What's left is the clean, exposed kernel. It drops down onto the waiting cloth or winnowing fan.

On a trip to India with my husband, we were driving through the countryside during the harvest. We often saw sheaves of grain strewn across dirt roads, the farmers hoping that a vehicle would come through and drive over the stalks, helping to prepare it for winnowing.

The metaphor of winnowing provides a beautiful image of the winds of God blowing away the chaff. The autumn wind carries away the chaff into the sky, into the sea of forgetfulness! The heart is the kernel, and this is what is most valuable and used for nourishment, especially when it's ground into flour and made into bread.

Once we endure this process with patience, we become like the leftover pieces of bread recovered by the disciples during the feeding of the five thousand. Broken, given, shared. We give of ourselves, love our neighbours, and share the good news as image-bearers of Christ.

The world we live in can feel hard. The war against our love and affection for God can be intense. Sometimes our hearts become hardened and calloused, just like the harvester's hands.

My self-talk in this season of winnowing was to encourage myself to allow God to come in and invade my comfort. To let Him disturb any sloth and complacency. To let his winds come through and blow upon my wrestling, crucified life. I welcomed the illumination of the Holy Spirit to expose the hidden things that kept me from prayer, from his presence and love. The chaff was any falsehood, deception, carelessness, rebellion, or resistance that hinders his love.

However, I've seen that we don't always want the chaff to be removed. Sometimes I like to protect myself with walls and layers in an attempt to keep me from pain. I don't always want to look at myself in the mirror; this is a human trait.

If we can be honest with God and ourselves, we will learn that our kneejerk reactions are meant to protect ourselves. I'm so thankful for the patience and kind mercy of God. He abides with us and helps us. He is right there, gathering us up and lighting the way. He is our loving companion in distress.

Through this winnowing, I learned to trust Him more. But before this measured growth, I found myself questioning, and sometimes isolating. I believed, but my life didn't always display the peace and rest I carried inside.

Regardless of why I had been wounded, He uncovered my heart's insecurities and affirmed my desire to worship God and need to be busy.

He also caused me to understand something about iron clamps. I think about Joseph from the Old Testament, who wore chains even though he was an innocent man. Joseph was imprisoned on false charges (Genesis 39, Psalm 105:16–19). Although completely innocent, he was thrown in prison without trial, without a voice, and without justice. He waited for three years to be released from his cell. Remarkably, he didn't harden his heart during the long wait; instead he turned his face to the Lord.

How fascinating and encouraging it is to read how this man behaved during his unlawful incarceration! Even there in the depth of darkness, God allowed Joseph to have favour, causing him to be appointed over all the other prisoners. He trusted God for his justice and freedom.

Joseph gives us another example of how we can live our lives in a manner that pleases God. We can excavate much gold in these precious seasons of our lives, recounting biblical stories of all the people who waited on God.

Abraham and Sarah waited for their promised son. Jacob waited for Rachel. Hannah waited for her promised son. So many people were forced to wait—Hezekiah, the apostle Paul, the woman with the issue of blood, Daniel, King David, Elijah, the Shulamite woman, and Anna and Simeon, just to name a few. Many of these men and women languished in personal solitude. They didn't have a blueprint, didn't know how long they would have to wait. They faced the great unknown.

As I ponder the many facets of my faith in Christ and knowledge of who God is, I've wondered, does the God of the universe allow the men of the earth to wrongly judge His children guilty, for a season, in order to test their faith? This is a hard and perplexing question. I've had to confront it throughout my life.

During the uninvited TBI, I found myself resisting the dealings of God. Had I forgotten about my eternal rewards? Had I overlooked the pure gold that can only come from the refining process? My flesh didn't want the winnowing. My flesh didn't desire the threshing floor.

But in the very depth of my soul, I thirsted and yearned to know Him, to be like Him, to be with Him. So I cried out to Jesus with the words of the Apostle Paul:

> [For my determined purpose is] that I may know Him [that I may progressively become more deeply and intimately acquainted with Him, perceiving and recognizing and understanding the wonders of His Person more strongly and more clearly], and that I may in

that same way come to know the power out-
flowing from His resurrection [which it exerts
over believers], and that I may so share His
sufferings as to be continually transformed
[in spirit into His likeness even] to His death,
[in the hope] that if possible I may attain to
the [spiritual and moral] resurrection [that
lifts me] out from among the dead [even
while in the body]. (Philippians 3:10–11)

This is my life's scripture. Time and time again,
these words rumble in my inner man, revealing my
spiritual cravings. Joined with this passion for Christ's
company is my intent to do the right thing, to be in
right relationship with everyone and always say yes to
my heavenly Father. God designed us with internal
spaces that only He can fill. When His Word is inside
us, we can only be fruitful.

I think back to Joseph and his heart's posture
upon being falsely charged. He wasn't indignant or
disobedient. So I take my turn and correct my gaze,
focusing on heaven, giving thanks to the Lord, for He
is good and His mercy endures forever.

When we develop spiritual maturity and allow
the Lord to have His way in us, we will focus on
what we can gain in spiritual riches, which transforms
our minds and wills to be in agreement with Christ.
Through the fire, we gain the knowledge of God.

In the book of Ephesians, the apostle Paul addresses the church in Ephesus:

> [For I always pray to] the God of our Lord Jesus Christ, the Father of glory, that He may grant you a spirit of wisdom and revelation [of insight into mysteries and secrets] in the [deep and intimate] knowledge of Him, by having the eyes of your heart flooded with light, so that you can know and understand the hope to which He has called you, and how rich is His glorious inheritance in the saints (His set-apart ones), and [so that you can know and understand] what is the immeasurable and unlimited and surpassing greatness of His power in and for us who believe, as demonstrated in the working of His mighty strength… (Ephesians 1:17–19)

We have a desire to know God as well as to be known by Him. Through this relationship, we sharpen our focus on eternal rewards and honouring Him, as opposed to taking the fast exit that causes us to harden our hearts. I pray, *Father, help me to bend my will to Yours. Grant me your spirit of wisdom and revelation that I may know you more deeply.*

When we understand that it's not about what happens to us, but rather how we respond to the heartfelt cry to follow the Lamb wherever He goes, we gain a clear and godly perspective. Of course, we would not choose the ways He chooses. We are comfort addicts. We look for the easiest, softest, most convenient way of doing things.

There are many lessons to learn from our trials. One thing we can count on is the door being opened to greater intimacy and deepening trust between us and the Father. With this comes a greater reliance on Him.

Allowing ourselves to be seen by others during these difficult seasons is a beautiful thing. People need to see that we aren't carrying the lingering, smoky bitterness on our garments. Our speech drips with love and peace, not fear and anxiety. Our eyes give us away, expressing who we've seen while in these most painful and trying flames.

That which was designed to destroy us becomes the very thing that exalts Christ, refines our faith, and fills us with mature love. Our light steadily brightens as our lives become a pleasing fragrance before God and others. Even our enemies will be at peace with us.

We will overcome, bearing witness again and again to the love and power of Christ in us, the hope of glory. We reveal His faithfulness and friendship. We bear the marks of suffering for all to see. We give ourselves and trust God with our lives. We are free indeed!

Even now, just as Jacob wrestled with the angel of the Lord who displaced his hip, I too walk at a different speed, my gait altered forever. The stride of the

Lord may not be what you and I imagine, and it may not line up with our past experiences, but it will always be the right way for us to walk. It will always line up with the scriptures—His way and His will, not mine.

I still have questions. Maybe they'll never be answered while I'm on this earth, but I can talk to God about it. His character never changes. He welcomes me to ask.

Furnace

Through life's difficulties, God enjoys seeing our faith. Faith is the currency of heaven and the battleground of the enemy, the sifting and shaking of all that can be. It is the loosening and brushing away of the hardness of the world, the throne of our souls, and the strongholds of deception, sloth, idolatry, and a divided heart—in short, sin, whatever needs to be blown away like the chaff at the threshing floor.

Here is where we go low as the winnowing hand of the Lord exposes all of our dead works in order to reveal what is true. May our hearts cry out, "Lord, show me truth that I may not be deceived!"

Let us recount the nail-biting story of Daniel's friends—namely, Shadrach, Meshach, and Abednego:

Shadrach, Meshach, and Abednego answered the king, O Nebuchadnezzar, it is not necessary for us to answer you on this point. If our God Whom we serve is able to deliver us from the burning fiery furnace, He will deliver us out of your hand, O king. But if not, let it be known to you, O king, that we will not serve your gods or worship the golden image which you have set up! Then Nebuchadnezzar was full of fury and his facial expression was changed [to antagonism] against Shadrach, Meshach, and Abednego. Therefore he commanded that the furnace should be heated seven times hotter than it was usually heated. And he commanded the strongest men in his army to bind Shadrach, Meshach, and Abednego and to cast them into the burning fiery furnace. Then these [three] men were bound in their cloaks, their tunics or undergarments, their turbans, and their other clothing, and they were cast into the midst of the burning fiery furnace. (Daniel 3:16–21)

These men had faith in God and didn't rely on political rescue. They were thrown into a flaming furnace so extreme in temperature that the guards were killed from the heat outside the mouth of the doorway.

For Daniel's friends, they did not insist that their lives be spared. On the contrary! They make no attempt to twist God's arm to get their own way. There is no begging, only complete dependence on God in a sure death as they relinquish any right to life. Their heart posture was one of full submission to God. They didn't even cry out for respite to end their suffering.

God spared their lives in a dramatic and supernatural account. This preincarnation of Christ is a powerful display of the omnipotence of God. But notice that the Lord didn't stand outside the mouth of the furnace, calling in, as the cowardly king had done. Instead He joined them in the fiery trial, literally

Consider that for a moment, or a lifetime. The Lord Himself entered these men's death sentence. In the same way, the Lord Himself entered the death sentence of all mankind.

As we read, God walks amidst the flames, releasing the captives' ropes and freeing them.

> Then Nebuchadnezzar the king [saw and] was astounded, and he jumped up and said to his counselors, Did we not cast three men bound into the midst of the fire? They answered, True, O king. He answered, Behold, I see four men loose, walking in the midst of the fire, and they are not hurt! And the form of the fourth is like a son of the gods! (Daniel 3:24–25)

Are we astonished when Jesus shows up in our circumstances? What is our expectation when everything seems hopeless? Jesus is the same yesterday, today, and forever!

Life often brings us to places where we are figuratively bound, but the presence of the Lord brings freedom and deliverance in the midst of trouble. He sets our minds and spirits free from all forms of bondage and imprisonment, even if things don't look like they're changing in the natural world.

There are many circumstances that don't change. But when we turn to God, and continue turning to Him with all our hearts, He gives us rest. You and I can hunker down into true heart-peace, because Jesus doesn't just *give* us peace; He *is* peace. His promises are boundless.

What amazing grace! Blessed are your eyes, for they will see wonders that those who lived before us could only dream of seeing.

Once delivered alive and well, the three men's clothing miraculously had no hint of the smell of smoke. No singed hair. No burns to the skin. No smoke damage to the lungs. Not even any residual bitterness. Everything about them was intact and fresh, speaking to their fully surrendered will to the Lord.

Have you ever felt like you've been burned? The Lord is the fourth man in your fire. Once you've been through the fire with Him, the fire will be kindled within you. It will burn with the incredible knowledge of the sweet fellowship of our suffering with our

Saviour Jesus Christ. Our battle cry will become, "Oh, that I might know Him!"

> Indeed, I count everything as loss because of the surpassing worth of knowing Christ Jesus my Lord. For his sake I have suffered the loss of all things and count them as rubbish, in order that I may gain Christ and be found in him, not having a righteousness of my own that comes from the law, but that which comes through faith in Christ, the righteousness from God that depends on faith… (Philippians 3:8–9, ESV)

These words of the apostle Paul are powerful and encouraging. As I began coming up for air from the intense symptoms of my concussion, I started to understand and see what I was gaining. We've all experienced many losses in life—in business, security, health, position, and finances. It counts as nothing in light of being found in Him.

I also felt the loss of my own righteousness, from making my own attempts to earn it, and in the end this resulted in an increase in faith.

It felt like an eternity before I was able to look again at my circumstances. It felt like a real resurrection, my body coming up out of the grave, like the love of the Lord when He kisses the morning with the rising sun to illuminate the earth. My one hope, my only hope, is in the One who said, "I am the resurrection!" He called my name, deep calling unto deep, bringing me out of the baptism waters of this living death. I am a prisoner of hope.

Prayerlessness

Losing my twin was excruciating, both physically and emotionally, and I was also living with an autoimmune condition and the pain of the concussion. But none of that compared to the deep, seemingly self-inflicted wound of my own prayerlessness in the aftermath of my injury; this was the most painful trial I ever experienced.

The road to healing was long and difficult, and sometimes I seemed to make little or no progress. But when your discipline and passion for prayer dries up, you suffer a different kind of pain—a pain that grows when you spend time away from the secret place. Loneliness, longing, and desire takes over.

Oh how I missed my Abba Father! How I yearned for His presence, His voice, His nearness. Everything was different in this new place. Cold. Isolating. It didn't seem like the road was ever going to be under my feet again.

I didn't recognize myself. It was like looking in the rear-view mirror, as though prayer and nearness with the Father were things of the past. This perspective brought a sense of hopelessness and despair, two things I was not accustomed to.

I struggled to move, stuck in quicksand. I gripped the kite string, hanging on for dear life. But the weight of the burden overcame me and I often found myself right back where I'd started, with no end in sight. Was this just the illusion of the enemy of my soul, deceiving me into thinking I was a failure, rejected by God? A life without prayer, a life without friendship and communion with God, is devastating to the human spirit. We were created to have fellowship with Jesus, walking and living in unity with Him.

Today I can say that recultivating a life of prayer, surrender, and rest is a daily choice. All I have to give God is my time. Time is all I have.

Our will is seated upon the throne of the heart, where emotions come and go and decisions are made. What will I do today with my will? How will I reconnect to my former lifestyle of prayer? I find some answers in Romans 8:26:

> So too the [Holy] Spirit comes to our aid and bears us up in our weakness; for we do not know what prayer to offer nor how to offer it worthily as we ought, but the Spirit Himself goes to meet our supplication and pleads in our behalf with unspeakable yearnings and groanings too deep for utterance.

The living Word of God provides the remedy to every question. Knowing and believing that the Holy Spirit goes to meet our prayers results in an overflowing measure of thanksgiving to Jesus. There is no room for striving or performance when we come to understand how God's Spirit works on our behalf in intercession and prayer.

The depth of Christ's pleading before the Father on our behalf provides closure to our doubts and misunderstandings about prayer and intimacy with God. Freedom can be found here and love is at work, coaxing us out of the desert and back into the land of the living.

Unbroken Fellowship

One day post-concussion as I read from scripture, the Lord highlighted something to me from 1 John 1:7:

> But if we [really] are living and walking in the Light, as He [Himself] is in the Light, we have [true, unbroken] fellowship with one another, and the blood of Jesus Christ His Son cleanses (removes) us from all sin and guilt [keeps us cleansed from sin in all its forms and manifestations].

Immediately, a broken relationship in my life came to my mind. I hadn't done anything other than to just let go and forget about it. When it comes to relational tensions, we tend to either confront immediately in order to clear the air or cross the street to avoid having to deal with it. We don't always choose to take a biblical approach, but I'm always willing to do the right thing, the very thing that would bless my Father.

One afternoon, while sitting outside in the warm spring sun, I had a casual chat with a neighbour. I tried to listen to her story of a family member who wanted to reconcile with her, but what she was saying had once again triggered a realization inside me, like that day when I had read from 1 John. It felt as if God Himself was giving me instructions, right then and there.

In that moment, I knew that I needed to make a move, to tie up loose ends with this person. I couldn't wait any longer.

I excused myself from the neighbour and went straight into the house to phone them. The action was abrupt. I moved quickly, so as not to counsel myself out of making the call. I had no idea what I would say, but after pacing the floor for five minutes I followed through.

The conversation was short, but in the tone of the other person's voice, I heard the sound of a burden rolling free.

The beauty of reconciliation is not having any agendas. I wasn't looking for anything from the offender; I just offered my voice to let them know that everything was okay. I needed to say hello and allow the Holy Spirit to wash off all the junk associated with our broken fellowship.

The enemy comes upon us with such negative thoughts. Even when you've forgiven another person, you may feel tempted to remain in the grips of unforgiveness. You may find yourself dwelling on that person's character flaws. Regardless, it's a dangerous state in which to live.

After that phone call, we both felt relief. The tension between us melted away. How easy it was to do this! There had been no pride, no demands or expectations. This simple act of reaching out had produced such freedom. It was a free gift! Thank You, Jesus.

It helps to remember that Christ didn't minimize the cost of the cross. He didn't try to lessen His own suffering, to make it easier on Himself, to make His situation more comfortable. One needn't exaggerate the unspeakable torture He endured at the hands of His tormenters, the very people He was paying the price for. It was the full price of my sins—of *our* sins.

We tend to diminish the horror of our sins, seeking to reduce the consequences when we're exposed. We want to soften the edges a bit, to talk that speeding ticket down. Reject and point fingers. Blame others. We make Christ more palatable for our mass consumption culture by downplaying sin. Yet with every attempt we dull the light that shines upon the freedom we have been graced through the finished work of the cross.

Nothing on earth compares to what Jesus, the man of sorrows, experienced in order to make a way for our lost world. Surely the suffering we face pales in comparison to anything He faced. Surely our light, momentary troubles are minute shadows when held close to His. Many of our afflictions are opportunities for us to be transformed into the image of the Son. What a privilege! What a divine glorious wonder it is that our lives are not our own, that He sees fit to reshape this measure of clay on the potter's wheel.

Francis Havergal is the nineteenth-century writer who wrote the old hymn "Take My Life and Let It Be." I love the lyrics she penned. They offer a prayer of hope and spiritual hunger for total consecration.

Take my life and let it be consecrated, Lord,
to thee. Take my moments and my days; let
them flow in endless praise, let them flow in
endless praise.[2]

There is beauty in losing one's life as we find our true life in Christ, a work that can only be completed through the Holy Spirit in us. Our lives are expressions of worship and endless prayer.

Humility

Charles Spurgeon once wrote, "I have learned to kiss the waves that throw me up against the Rock of Ages."[3]

Well, in this difficult season of my life, I learned to kiss the waves that rocked me.

Sometimes we feel shipwrecked, trapped, pummelled, and buried inside the collapse of our "normal" lives. Perhaps we're here for an extended season of separation from life as we knew it, life as we want it to be. However long the season, learning to live in the here and now is crucial.

Our minds are a battleground for hope and faith. Like me, maybe you cry out, "Oh Lord, I believe, but help my unbelief!" If this is your cry, so be it. He's not an idol that cannot hear or see; He is the living God, El Roi, who is touched by our weaknesses and trouble while creating something beautiful in us through it, expanding our ability to lean into Him alone as our rock.

Affliction can temper our hearts quite efficiently. When we neglect the condition of our souls, our hearts and minds grow hard and stubborn. Suffering and pain can be useful, forcing us to surrender ourselves to Christ.

This can be a catalyst for us to dig into the fallow ground of our hearts, to prepare for the seeding of God's precepts, cultivating and nurturing what has already been planted. Seeds can land in good soil that's ready and waiting for His teachings of divine love, allowing us to receive the water that will produce fruit in our lives, fruit that lasts. This is the eternal treasure of our heavenly Father.

Our lives don't stop because of circumstances that produce major changes. Our lives continue forward as we grow desperate for relief. When we factor in the value of what Christ suffered, we more greatly value what He takes us through on the earth in our distress and woe.

In the year after my concussion, my inability to form coherent thoughts and sentence was most challenging. There were so many cognitive malfunctions. My speech was often disconnected, my words strung together in wild ways.

It was a strange experience navigating thoughts and speech that didn't come together naturally. I could think of an object but not remember its name. In conversation, I'd look off to the side as my brain rapidly searched for a word. What on earth were we talking about? This sometimes brought on stumbling embarrassment.

I discussed these symptoms with my neurologist multiple times as I wiped tears from the corner of my eyes.

"I used to be smart," I'd say with an uneasy guffaw, squirming in discomfort. "Now I sound stupid, like I have a disability. It's humiliating."

It was a harsh reality, but the doctor heard these grievances often enough to respond well. He nudged me along to truth and acceptance, assuring me that this was all part of the pilgrimage, that we're all just commoners taking the low road.

The idea that people would perceive me as slow was humbling. But maybe it would be more honest to say that it felt like an injustice. I hated having to struggle to find words for ordinary concepts. We tend to hold tightly to our strengths and hope they cover our weaknesses.

When we're in the middle of a trial, we are confronted by surprises, such as when our hidden pride pokes out to say hello. It's a very unwelcome visitor. I counsel myself that there can be no room for pride in my life, that I must accept the weakness and allow the Lord to work out whatever needs to be done. Then I remind myself that this is all worth it, because Jesus is worth it.

The apostle Paul writes,

But he said to me, "My grace is sufficient for you, for my power is made perfect in weakness." Therefore I will boast all the more gladly of my weaknesses, so that the power of Christ may rest upon me. (2 Corinthians 12:9, ESV)

I mess up often. There are misunderstandings. I say the wrong things. I sometimes approach people the wrong way. It might come across as rude, but that's not my intent. I just have no filter and don't know how to fix it.

Even when I'm thoughtful and slow, the process of pressing out words can be like ingesting sour wine. I sometimes speak impulsive words that haven't been vetted in the discernment compartment of my brain. Afterward I apologize with a big sigh.

And so it continues. I wrongly approach a saleswoman about an item in the store. I return to apologize. She tells me that all is forgiven, yet she won't speak to me and makes dismissive gestures, even though we live on the same street and she's a believer.

Humility is a narrow way.

Oh, but recall the joy of Christ in our times of great trouble! Humility goes a long way. I try to remember that. I just have to train myself to go there first, to humility, to choose the low road, to quiet myself and regain the mind of Christ in all things. I must refocus, rethink, and revive myself in the words of Christ and His teachings. I need to beat that old nature to death!

Remember, you're a disciple of Christ. You are His follower, and following Him means gaining understanding and insight into what He teaches you. Trust and obey. Love. I must decrease; He must increase. This is my identity.

When I don't know what to do, I can always recalibrate and say, "I may not know now what to do or what will happen, but what do I know? I know God is good. His mercy is new every morning. He has chosen me and has loved me with an everlasting love. I know

I can trust Him fully with my life. I know He is faithful. I know He is just. I know He leads me beside still waters. I know He lives and is the great intercessor, making intercession for me. I know He is my protector and good Father. He is the author and finisher of my faith, the lover of my soul. He purchased me with His own blood and gives me new life. I know His Holy Spirit comes to meet my prayers, crying out on my behalf with groans too deep for words."

I weep in gratitude.

And he said to them, "Come away by yourselves to a desolate place and rest a while." For many were coming and going, and they had no leisure even to eat. (Mark 6:31, ESV)

III

Enter into Solitude

Regulating one's life during and after a trauma can be challenging. Those closest to us may not understand the extent of our difficulty. It's easier to downplay the agony, and perhaps even ignore it.

We can find fellowship with Christ in suffering. Many of us miss out on this fellowship, though, because of our great resistance. We are quick to reach for the painkiller, anything that numbs us and keeps us moving beyond the point where the Lord may want us to stop. We divert ourselves to keep order and keep things comfortable. Don't change anything please.

What might the Father be inviting me into during my season of adversity? What have I missed just because I wanted to get out of it and push the exit button? What does our Father say about suffering? Could this be an invitation to consecrate ourselves to the Lord for a time?

The idea of solitude can terrify us according to our western, modern ways of thinking. But setting aside some dedicated time of prayer and waiting on the Lord is crucial for our spiritual health and growth. How can we know Christ if we're too busy to stop and sit with Him? We can be led into the proverbial desert, where we have no option but to sit and wait in our quiet interlude.

Some people are very uncomfortable being alone, perhaps even tormented by the prospect. Maybe you're one of those people who finds it painful to eat by yourself at a restaurant, for example, or be home alone. So you ensure that there's constant noise, such as music or the TV playing in the background.

In our culture, we're bombarded with sights and sounds that fight for our attention. Our eyes always have something to look at, some colourful, blinking, tempting message. Flashing billboards, mobile phones, and endless social media feeds assault our senses every second of the day, threatening our contentment and enticing us into deeper consumerism.

It's very difficult to find solitude. Even in the dark of night, people are out working, travelling, eating, gaming, and watching movies. It seems as if the world never stops. People are continually on the move.

This nonstop culture only emphasizes the need for us to create a space where we can intentionally stop, set ourselves apart, and get quiet—not solely for the purpose of being quiet, but of being able to encounter the One who waits for us. He will meet us there, in the quiet, as we make the effort. He is very kind. And if you haven't discovered this yet, you will.

There must be something more to this solitude if our world aggressively opposes it. Perhaps it's been your mindset not to permit yourself to take a break, or maybe you are so driven that you don't allow for downtime. Seeking rest and stillness allows us to create a personal culture of meditative, intentional prayer. In this type of prayer place, we can hear God much better than when we're running round the hamster wheel.

We need to cultivate our own culture of prayer, one that hews closer to the rhythms of our lives—the beating of wings, the pulse flushing our veins, the breath in our lungs, and the rhythm of our weeping. But instead we overwork, putting in extra hours at our jobs and not giving ourselves permission to take a break to care for our spiritual needs. We feel guilty for stopping.

Once we release ourselves, we discover that the false guilt imposed on us by the world has one purpose: to keep us caught up in our cares and pressures, preventing us from pressing in for a deeper walk with Jesus and going beyond the complacency of church life. We need to remove all this guilt, even when it's self-imposed.

In my early days as a follower of Christ, I bought into the lie that says "If you stop, you're no longer a healthy contributor to society or your family." It's a subtle lie. It sets us up to chase perfection, which leads to disappointment and even self-loathing. When we follow the world's patterns, we essentially reject God's invitation for us to come away with Him and get to know Him better. Jesus longs for us to sit at his feet, as Mary learned to do while her sister Martha was occupied with serving.

My brain wound has caused me to develop a quiet, contemplative lifestyle which, I believe, is by the Lord's design. If we neglect studying the Bible and prayer, we neglect the intimacy that arises from a thankful heart that has been forgiven much.

Strangely, however, I couldn't read or pray along my healing journey. Instead my prayers took the form of inaudible thoughts and cries of the heart.

Poustinia

What is a poustinia? This Russian word, translated simply, means *desert*. The connotation is a quiet, lonely place which people may enter to meet God. It's a physical place of isolation and seclusion from the noisy flush of the world.

Historically, we can see this through the Desert Fathers, early believers in Christ who lived ascetic life-styles. They left busy towns and cities in order to settle in desolate places, creating opportunities to get away with God.

The same trend is slowly becoming popular again in today's culture.

A poustinia retreat would be a small, simple build-ing with only a chair and perhaps a plain bed. There were no distractions. People would enter this desert place without any belongings other than the clothes on their back, a Bible, and some bread and water.

In such a place, we can wrestle in fasting, prayer, and intercession. We grapple with our thoughts, our need to relax, our mental exhaustion. Fears of being alone may overwhelm us as our thoughts clash loudly. We fight to settle in, battling for the stillness that so often eludes us.

In her book, *Poustinia*, Catherine Doherty writes,

> To go into the Poustinia means to listen to God. It means entering into kenosis-the emptying of oneself. This is really a climbing of this awesome mountain right to the very top where God abides in his warm silence. It also means to know how terrible it is to

fall into the hands of the living God, and yet how delightful, how joyful, how attractive! So attractive, in fact, that the soul cannot resist.[4]

God speaks to us all the time through scripture, the preaching and teaching of His words, prayer, and many other means as He so chooses. The weeks I spent in concussion lockdown were a kind of poustinia. Just like the appeal to enter into His joy, Jesus calls us out of anxious worry to come to Him, our life's remedy.

But how do we find our own desert shack to retreat to?

In our society, we are quick to avoid taking time to just listen. We often don't want to hear words and be comforted, encouraged, and taught by God's voice—not your own inner voice, but that of the divine holy Father who invites us to come away with Him.

Being still and quiet doesn't have to be awkward or uncomfortable. It will be, at first, for anyone who's stepping out in this way for the first time. That's perfectly okay. It takes practice and discipline. I had to reconcile my normal, hectic way of being and hunker down into true sabbath rest. Sometimes it makes me feel old, but I've since discovered the consistent and dependable desert that burns within me.

We seldom hear the words "Take your time. There's no rush." But as we learn to reorder our steps, we may find that our stride changes, slowing down to the point that we become more aware of the fire within us, the yearning to abide with Jesus.

The physical place where we wait is important. By establishing a chair, a corner, or any place marked for prayer and contemplation, we help to create a new habit. I had to consciously make my life a prayer once again, and it took effort.

Henri Nouwen offers us a beautiful invitation to enter into solitude with Christ, even in the midst of adversity:

> Solitude is the furnace of transformation. Without solitude we remain victims of our society and continue to be entangled in the illusions of the false self.[5]

To enter solitude is to be stripped of our devices and all the busyness of life that prevents us from knowing God in a more intimate way. It's much more than unplugging from society, though. The voice we will hear isn't the same one we hear in the world, the one that comes from just vegging out and mindlessly binging movies and TV shows according to the social structures of the culture around us.

Once again, Henri Nouwen describes it well:

> But that is not the solitude of St John the Baptist, of St. Anthony or St Benedict, of Charles de Foucauld or the brothers of Taizé.

> For them solitude is not a private therapeutic place. Rather, it is the place of conversion, the place where the old self dies and the new self is born, the place where the emergence of the new man and the new woman occurs… The struggle is to die to the false self.[6]

I love this conversion, when the old is put away and the new comes. The Holy Spirit brings reformation to the heart of every man. Thanks be to God!

The fires of our lives have a purpose: to make us aware of all the falsehoods we have believed about ourselves and God. This includes false pride masquerading as humility. We scream out for God to keep us from all forms of struggle and pain only to discover that we are aiming to twist the God of creation into something small and palatable, a form of godliness we deem good and right.

In these troubled waters, we have the opportunity to press into God in prayer. We draw near to Him and he draws near to us. So many times I've tried hard to live normally when it was simply impossible, considering my injury. We simply can't do it. We can't escape the dealings of the Lord. When we welcome His hand, there is much to gain.

In our healing, we are often told to wait. Healing takes time. Bones need to knit back together, muscles need to unravel, brains need rest, and broken hearts require wisdom and the balm of the Lord, which He has given liberally to His church. We cannot go about our day-to-day lives and ignore suffering. We need the body of Christ, which is called to love and serve one another. We wait on the Lord. He is faithful.

While I was on a mission trip in Uganda and Kenya, everything we did took much longer than we were used to in western culture. The locals used a common phrase: "Hurry up and wait."

This captures how I feel during periods of unexpected waiting. Delays when the car is in for repairs, or when I stand in line for coffee or at the grocery checkout. We wait impatiently. Waiting too long can be a terrible problem for us.

I have so much respect for Jonah. Imagine his horror at being swallowed up by a huge fish and lodged deep inside for three days—the stomach acids, the smell of rotting fish, the compression from the walls of the belly, the regurgitation, the swirling and rolling movement... terrifying. It took three days of prayer, and the prospect of death, to reset his heart towards God in obedience.

He was stubborn, and sometimes I can be too. Our Father is patient and oh so kind towards us, pouring out gracious love to those like me who are undeserving.

When the tests come and we feel hemmed in, we immediately get anxious and wonder what we've done wrong. Maybe we even believe that God is punishing us.

It's imperative to have the right view of God.

The belly of the whale is a dark place and it might instill fear, instability, panic, depression, and doubt. But since we have the whole story concerning Jonah, we can see that the Lord protected him and orchestrated the situation to help turn his heart toward obedience.

I wonder how many times in our lives the Lord has kindly nudged us in this same way while we felt he was punishing us. The truth is that we don't understand His ways. Perhaps we even give credit to the devil. Can we recalibrate how we see God in times of trouble?

Retreat

Just over a year after my head injury, wanting to get away and spend some uninterrupted time with God, I booked myself into a silent retreat. It was hard. There was no talking, not even at mealtimes. That was sad for me.

I spent a lot of time in my cozy single bedroom overlooking a snow-covered, pine-filled acreage along the beautiful shores of Lake Ontario. Sipping my hot tea with honey, I snuggled into the rocking chair as the large windows and warm radiators helped me feel tucked into God.

Earlier in the day I had a meeting with my spiritual director. She was a good sounding board. However, later that afternoon the Holy Spirit spoke to me while

I rocked on that dusty rose chair. While I bemoaned to the Lord about a heart wound, He clearly impressed these words to me: "Deny yourself."

I knew immediately what he was saying: "Deny yourself the right to anger over this hurtful injustice. Pick up your cross and follow me."

Jesus denied Himself the right to life, the right to conquer and retaliate against the injustice done to Him. Instead He turned the other cheek, literally. He denied himself His rights. Then, as clear as a bell, I was impressed with these words: "Let them get away with it."

Really? I wondered, like the dumb-dumb I sometimes am.

The Holy Spirit quickly reminded me that He had freely forgiven me whenever I asked in repentance. It was a quick work of release. Thank God! His words felt like a hot brand pressed into the flesh of my heart. In this unforgettable moment, I was marked once again by His love and mercy.

Our conversations with Jesus are like the ones He had with His disciples. We are His friends, as they were. We may sit beside someone who has hurt us— and when we repent and offer forgiveness, we receive the same. How mature and healthy would the body of Christ be if we sat together actively forgiving each other and extending repentance?

I think about this often. Instead we isolate ourselves from our offenders. Instead of drawing near in reconciliation, we recoil. We cross the street to avoid the discomfort of confrontation. We nurture and protect our wounds as if there were no remedy.

When did our feelings become so important, so coddled, so protected? Is society to blame? Is forgiveness really that difficult? If so, why is that?

There is a subtle mind shift the church uses to justify unforgiveness, taking offence, and holding grudges.

"I can forgive, but I can't forget," some people proclaim.

"But you don't know what they did to me!" others insist. "He doesn't deserve to be let off the hook. It's unforgivable!"

The grace of God is immeasurable. These statements are wrong in any variation. We need to repent and get things right with the Lord.

I once heard a preacher talk about forgiveness. He spoke about the fact that no matter the trespass, no matter how terrible that hurt or how it came about, we must forgive. Why? Because even if we can justify our unforgiveness a hundred ways, we're still wrong.

Even if we're right, we're wrong.

It's an excellent point. Our unwillingness to cancel debts not only is wrong, but it's sin. Jesus said it very clearly:

But if you do not forgive others their trespasses [their reckless and willful sins, leaving them, letting them go, and giving up resentment], neither will your Father forgive you your trespasses. (Matthew 6:15)

This is a battleground for us. Jesus paid the price, completely forgiving our debt, and it's a debt we cannot repay.

So when someone commits an offence against you, let them get away with it. After all, God let you and me "get away" with that enormous debt of ours. Those who love much have been forgiven much. Let us be those who are forgiven much, extending continual liberty to all who have hurt us. Let us also love much. Laying down our will isn't just an act of obedience; it's a response of love that eliminates the stubborn areas of our hearts and exposes our true beliefs about God.

Old Paths

What does it look like to return to one's old paths? For me, these paths have included practical ways of life such as taking personal retreats, studying the scriptures, serving, hospitality, plunking on my guitar in worship, reading and praying liturgy, prayer-walking, fasting, and attending prayer groups and other meetings.

When we're knocked off-course, it can seem impossible to regain our former spiritual disciplines. But we don't give up, and we don't stop trying to establish rhythms of prayer and worship. These rhythms are our lifeline to God, our privilege as His children, and our legal right as citizens of heaven. We humble ourselves, go low, and take note of the lowly servant, Jesus. We wash the feet of others, open ourselves to hospitality, and preach the good news that we have been forgiven of our sins because He paid the price and purchased us. Glory in His goodness! Pray out loud! Get out of your own head! Read His words back to Him! Engage and delight yourself in the Lord! Sing a new song! Throw your cares back upon the Lord, like the fishermen casting heavy nets into the sea!

As A.W. Tozer once wrote, "The neglected heart will soon be a heart overrun with worldly thoughts. The neglected life will soon become a moral chaos."[7]

Prayer

Oh, whistling Shepherd,
Blow your breath-wind through the air
'Til it awakens hear in me,
Sounding through the narrow way
Into my heart this sound obey

When I awoke on the twelfth day after my injury, I was finally able to pray out loud again. I cannot express the joy I experienced when I was able to collect and connect thoughts in this way through a small prayer.

My words were simple, my speech halted: "God, I ask for Your protection over the women in my family. Every generation." This year had brought so many suddenlies that seemed to directly affect the women in my family: untimely death, broken bones, head injuries, surgeries, etc. So this was my prayer. Nothing fancy, just what was needed. Oftentimes these are the experiences that teach us how to pray. No striving.

Sometimes we feel defeated in our attempts to pray. When we compare ourselves with others, we come up short.

Prayer has been at the core of my existence since my spirit was reborn into Christ's kingdom. Yielding my time in prayer to God, as well as having a mature spiritual mentor, helped me to cultivate a life of prayer. My involvement in prayer movements and ministries has also trained me in prayer.

But here I was, praying out loud for the first time in days. A person listening might have responded, "Is that it?" It's easy to fall into performance mode while praying, especially if you receive accolades and pats on the back. These types of prayers are directed more at others than God.

Throughout the winnowing process, God may need to remove some performance chaff. Our weak prayers, our simple words, and even our breath prayers are precious to our heavenly Father.

Prayer is our altar of sweet smelling incense that wafts up to God. Prayer and worship smoulder in the coals of our spirits, hearts, and mouths. Drawing from the pure oil of His Spirit, our hearts are the wick and His presence the oil. We exalt the Lord with song, shouts, and quiet gratitude. We worship Him because He alone is worthy to receive it.

I admit that there have been seasons in my life when it seemed as though my altar was impoverished and cold. No embers or coals. No fragrant spices to burn before the One who rightly deserves it.

That's a painful place to find oneself! Yet we were created for worship and communion with the Father. When we enter the fields of suffering, we may find ourselves in this place—unable to walk in the gardens of thanksgiving or fields of praise.

Many things can steal our gaze from the throne of God. We must be diligent in divorcing ourselves from sloth, selfishness, and vain imaginations. Our difficulties should move us toward God and into prayer and praise.

Without the altar of incense alive in our inner lives, we will find ourselves burning strange things, wrong doctrines, and pseudo-Christianity. We may worship with our lips only, our hearts far from Him. May it never be so.

The soul in need learns to press into God in prayer, pressing past the breaking point toward breakthrough. The Holy Spirit leads us and empowers us. When we give ourselves in the place of prayer, He helps us to endure until we come through. Our greatest reward is recognizing that He is whom we need most, and then pressing in until it is He whom we have most.

Little Bird

After Marni passed away in early January 2019, our family had the difficult task of going through some of her personal effects. She had saved everything. Gifts she had been given years prior were still in their original packages, put in a drawer or left in a safe place but never used.

Marni didn't put much value in material things and always lived a very simple life, focused more on enjoying a good novel, cooking up gourmet food, or going out to her favourite dim sum restaurant.

While we looked through her jewellery stash, much to my joy I found a sweet copper necklace I had given her the year before on our birthday. A small songbird hung from the simple chain, an artisanal piece purchased in a local craft boutique. It had reminded me of her—quiet, unassuming, preferring the covered tree branches, safely hidden in the shadows.

God had impacted me with this find by allowing me to see something encouraging in the image of the songbird.

Birds are often difficult to spot, as they camouflage themselves well. This is for their own safety. We often don't notice a little bird sitting near us until it opens its beak and begins to sing. We're generally unaware that birds are all around us, flying overhead, nesting, and foraging for food.

I cried when I put the necklace on for the first time. I felt like that little copper bird. Seemingly insignificant. Out of sight, out of mind. Alone on a branch or a ledge, quietly waiting, watching, wondering when it would be safe.

After the head injury, I wore this necklace to remind myself that one day my song would return and it would be spring again.

During times of confinement, we can feel so tiny and powerless, especially when we can't do the things we normally would. Vulnerability reflects back at us and we feel broken, shattered, and weak. There's an internal struggle, with our inner voice declaring, "Be a valiant warrior! You can do it!" This part of us attempts to take control, to jump up and overcome it all. Victory! It wants us to *do something*, even when every bone in our body has been crushed.

That push to act is a force we need to reckon with.

The voice of the bird and its song is worship to God, and music to me. It's such a small creature—until it sings. Then melodies float on the air.

Every time I see that necklace, I'm reminded about how fragile life is. But even during painful times of waiting, there is a song being sung somewhere. God is writing on the tablets of our hearts. His song is for us. It's a new song, to be sung in the perfect timing of this journey we're on. Even if it's only you and the Father who ever hear it, or sing it, it will be lifegiving.

This bird speaks of solitude and the comfort that can be found tucked away in Christ. It's not a scary place; it's a solid space where one can listen, wait with expectation, and linger with a hopeful heart that God will speak. He will lead. He is near. No secret keys required.

How often do we stop to find a place of solitude for meditative prayer, a place to wait on God? But we feel the pressure to do something, anything, as long as it's not nothing.

It's important to redefine "nothing." For example, consider the sabbath. Finding true sabbath rest isn't about weighing in on how much we can and can't do, but about strengthening our eternal connection to God. The sabbath "nothing" is something of eternal substance.

Coming through my TBI, I began to ask myself, what is humility and why does God bless it? We know that the Lord opposes the proud and welcomes those who are meek. He teaches us, *"Let each regard the others as better than and superior to himself"* (Philippians 2:3). And he also shows us that our identity is married to our pride: *"He must increase, but I must decrease"* (John 3:30). And we read in 1 Peter 5:5,

> Clothe (apron) yourselves, all of you, with humility [as the garb of a servant, so that its

covering cannot possibly be stripped from you, with freedom from pride and arrogance] toward one another.

This is humility. This canopy of clothing is freedom from pride and arrogance. It's a form of demoting oneself for the good of others. When we become like Christ, we become humble in all we say and do, including how we treat others.

Let us humble ourselves before God and not ask Him to humble us. Let's choose to go low, and lower still, until our lives truly are not our own, but Christ's alone. We choose the wrappings of lowliness. We choose to be like Him by, dare I say, being average in the eyes of the world.

The posture of my heart is the posture the Lord sees. Being comfortable on my knees before God is a good thing. It causes our hearts and attitudes to follow into a posture of intentional humility.

> If I sit and do nothing
> Nothing but pray,
> What have I done?
> If all I can do is nothing,
> Nothing but pray,
> What have I done?

But this I call to mind, and therefore I have hope: the steadfast love of the Lord never ceases; his mercies never come to an end; they are new every morning; great is your faithfulness. "The Lord is my portion," says my soul, "therefore I will hope in him." (Lamentations 3:21–24, ESV)

IV

What to Do?

The neurologist prescribed walking every day as part of my rehabilitation. Incremental daily activity was important, he said, and indeed getting out the front door was getting easier every day.

However, trying to walk around the block was a longer process. Sunglasses and earplugs were my constant companions.

We would start with my husband walking with me to the house next door, then coming right back home.

The next day, we would walk past two driveways. Each day, I had to walk to an additional house.

I remember the first time I walked around the whole block. My brain went into the red zone rather quickly, which was normal at this point. These full-blown meltdowns were regular occurrences.

Throughout this season of tossing and turning, there were times when I would get up and try to move around the house. I'd look for something small to do, something to move me out of pain and distress.

One day I noticed a polishing cloth. Taking some silver jewellery in hand, I began to slowly clean it. It was strange to move my limbs undertaking such a mindless job. After finishing just one necklace and a pair of earrings, I was done. The task gave me a measurement of how far I still had to go down this road of recovery. I had to remind myself that this was not a race.

Two months post-concussion, I sat in my car for the first time. I positioned myself behind the steering wheel, my hand resting on the stick shift, and looked around the driveway. My senses were completely overwhelmed and my heartrate sped up.

The next day, I tried it again, but this time I started the car. Elation rose within me, but the brain panic was close behind. Jesus, help me!

The next day, I drove down the driveway and backed up. A neighbour pretended she wasn't looking, but still managed to catch my eye. I chuckled. What a wild day.

The following week, I drove down the street and back.

Step by step, day by day, those measured exercises taught me to keep going. They reminded me how important the disciplines of faith were to me.

Finally, I was able to drive around the block.

Incremental recovery. Discipline. Every day, there was something more I had to do—charting my every move, recording the meltdowns, the yellow zones, the red zones. I was vulnerable but trying. Building but retreating. I had so many emotional responses that I couldn't decipher them all. Joy, fear, panic, nausea, hope… dizziness, migraines, grief, neck pain…

God was with me through all of it.

My journal entries from this period are full of thankful prayers and meditations on my distress and fellowship with Christ. They include words and poetry, laments and worship. It was a beautiful disaster, but somehow it all made sense and even had a sweet harmony that played out in my day-to-day life.

"What are my expectations?" I wrote. "Healing? God reminds me of how weak I am, but also how powerful and mighty he is. Oh, I boast in my weakness so the power of Christ may rest upon me. May Christ be seen in this time, this recovery, this pain."

There was fight and surrender, flight and acceptance, disappointment and clarity. These were the songs of my life relinquishing its own ways.

Get Oil

What does it look like to seek? What does it feel like? With all our seeking, we find the common thread of hearts turning to God again and again in pursuit of His voice and presence. It's about pursuing the desire to know Him more and behold Him. We long to gain a greater revelation of the Son of God. We pursue by seeking to hear Him, to gaze upon His beauty and give ourselves away over and over again, to be transformed from the self to the glorious light of His presence in our lives.

We seek You, Lord God, yet You have sought us out and we have been found by You. This is the heart quest of every follower of Christ. We search You out as the unsearchable and glorious Father of lights, our good God who fills us with the oil of His presence.

By August, the summer was hot. Fry-an-egg-on-a-car hot. We had opened our cottage and I parked myself there for five weeks. I found another kind of solitude there and didn't want to leave.

Every night I read out of a little book called *Revival in the Hebrides* by Duncan Campbell.[8] I would then feel the inner stirrings of the Spirit of God and found it hard to sleep. In the mornings, I'd turn my thoughts and prayer to the Lord and ask Him about revival, about how asking and seeking go together.

I knew that revival would signal the return of King Jesus and I wanted oil in my lamp. I wanted to be found ready when our Jesus returns to the earth. I'm serious about this, just as Jesus was.

In Matthew 25, Jesus told a parable that teaches us the gravity of the hour. He explained that a midnight cry would one day awaken the espoused bride of Christ, who is to wait for Him, prepared with extra oil for her lamp. The ten waiting virgins, representing believers, all fell asleep. But when they awoke at the announcement of the arrival of the groom, only half of them were prepared. Only five had oil in their lamps and were ready to go.

The singer-songwriter Harvest Bashta sings "Make Us Ready," a poignant song I've been listening to lately. She sings, "Let there be oil in my lamp. Let the fire not go out. When I hear the Bridegroom comes, make us ready."[9]

Are we ready for the return of our Bridegroom? The book of Revelation ends with this: *"The [Holy] Spirit and the bride (the church, the true Christians) say, Come!"* (Revelation 22:17) What is the spirit of the church of Christ saying? What does your spirit say to your Bridegroom today?

Every January, my faith community comes together for a focused time of prayer and fasting. One year, the Lord impressed upon me these words: "Get oil." Since then, I had been flapping my broken wings in an attempt to get more oil, in the only way I could understand.

I felt a sense of emptiness as I positioned myself before the Lord, waiting. My post-concussion brain still didn't allow me to maintain a coherent train of thought for long, and this felt like yet another failed attempt.

But there I was, at the cottage, looking out the bug-speckled window, leaning my elbows on my old writer's desk. I studied all the shells and sea glass lined up on the windowsill. I admired the white coral branch I had picked up during some long forgotten seaside stroll. There was the tiny, perfectly formed conch shell from South Caicos, and the brilliant white quartz stone I'd found just down the road at Flatrock.

Everyone who stays here knows about Flatrock. It's the perfect place to enter the chilly waters, and it sits at the end of the cottage lined road. Here, swimmers can walk atop the exposed surface of the rock and step into the lake for a refreshing dip.

I gazed out at the massive body of water that is Lake Ontario pushing and pulling me. I read from my Bible and then listened. I asked the Father to give me a fresh desire for His kingdom, and new eyes with which to enter a place of prayer to draw from the oil that fills our ongoing need to burn for Christ.

This was the same oil the widow of 2 Kings kept in her home when the creditors tried to take her young sons as bond payment for what her dead husband owed. Had that oil been left from her husband, who was a prophet? In 2 Kings 4, Elisha arrived after the widow called for him. The oil began to flow, filling every empty jar or vessel her sons could get their hands on. When they were full, the oil ceased. As long as there were empty containers, there was plenty of oil to fill them. Hallelujah!

But what is this oil we read about in the Bible? Where do we get it and what does it cost?

Symbolically, oil represents the Holy Spirit, the presence of God. It was used to anoint kings, heal the sick, and treat wounds. It was mixed in food, poured out as offerings, and even used in perfumes and burial ointments.

Oil also played a part in tabernacle worship. The golden lampstand was fed with oil to keep the lights burning perpetually. The tabernacle priests were responsible for keeping the lampstand burning by regularly replenishing its oil supply.

This presents a beautiful picture and reminder that we, as priests of Christ, minister before the Lord and keep the oil of our faith full and our wicks glowing brightly, shining light into the dark world in which we live. I'm reminded of the words of the apostle Paul:

> But in a great house there are not only vessels of gold and silver, but also [utensils] of wood and earthenware, and some for honorable and noble [use] and some for menial and ignoble [use]. So whoever cleanses himself [from what is ignoble and unclean, who separates

himself from contact with contaminating and corrupting influences] will [then himself] be a vessel set apart and useful for honorable and noble purposes, consecrated and profitable to the Master, fit and ready for any good work. (2 Timothy 2:20–21)

When I was twenty-six years old, it was midday and my firstborn was down for her nap. I sat at the kitchen table with my Bible open to 2 Timothy. With my spirit gripped upon this passage, I was deeply moved to discover that God's transforming power is available to me as his daughter.

Gnawing hunger clutched my spirit-belly. I dropped my eyes and spoke with great intensity: "Jesus, I want to be a vessel of gold. Make me a vessel of honour. Jesus, make me a vessel of gold… it's my desire to be a vessel of honour…"

Suddenly, I heard the audible voice of the Lord. It scared me! My body jumped and my eyes flashed wide as I looked around the room. The Lord's response swiftly hits my ears: "Are you willing to be emptied first?"

"Yes," I heard myself say. "Yes!"

But terror gripped me as I was overtaken by the fear of the Lord.

What does this mean? Was something bad going to happen to me? What does it mean to be emptied? I was deeply afraid that I had said yes without knowing what it would mean for me and my family. I hadn't counted the cost. I was young in the faith and didn't fully grasp that God had much to teach me.

As my day carried on, I felt the awe of the Lord upon me.

When the day came to an end, I laid down in bed and said, "Lord, I surrender to You my yes... but I'm afraid, because I don't know what it means. I know what I want and that is to be a vessel of honour, a vessel of gold. This is what I want. I'm scared, but go ahead and empty me."

Throughout my life, this emptying has turned out to be an ongoing, seasonal refining. Sometimes I'm more aware of it than others. It might be fair to say that there comes a purging of the self, a sort of death like we see with the arrival of winter. Afterward we are tempted to replace that which has been purged with the self again. But there is too much *me*, too much *you*.

It's really quite simple. Like stones rolling on the ocean floor, we come to the light only to be pulled back under the current. So we roll forward and back again in this awkward struggle to stay in the light. As we are turned back and forth, the edges and corners grow smooth and rounded. The waves drag us around until we're softer than when we started. Eventually, we gain our footings and are no longer tossed about at the world's commands; we find that we are more like Christ. Perhaps it takes the ocean to help us know the power we already possess in Him.

The waterfront view out the window of my cottage was crashing and loud and constantly in motion. I could never contain it. But the Spirit of God wants full possession of us. He makes it possible for us to be carriers of His glory, His presence, His Spirit. Like the fullness of the oceans, Christ's fullness is contained within His flesh and blood.

We are human beings walking the earth as sons and daughters of oil (Zechariah 4:14). Like the magnificent power that pulls the waves across the face of the earth, believers carry the spirit of Christ in our inner beings, the promise of God that we are now part of His family, His kingdom. I can't explain it, but it's true.

This is what it looked like to ask and seek during this broken season of my life. I asked continually, aloud, in my heart and mind, in song, in tongues of angels, desiring to be a vessel of honour and gold. I asked the Lord to revive my spirit. I waited and asked and looked for Him.

I thought back on moments from the past, of dreams, visions, and things forgotten or lost—even things found. He has reminded me that there are no works I can do to earn this. Instead He takes pleasure in giving good gifts to His children.

So I wait and give myself time to realign my crooked paths of thinking and posture myself in humility, allowing space for myself to become aware of His transforming power at work in me and to say thank You. Thank You for loving me first. Thank You for being the Lord and creator of all things. Thank You for giving me the mind of Christ and a heart that seeks after You. Thank You for Your abundant goodness, Your forgiveness of sins, Your healing power, and Your unchanging love. Thank You for making Your home within our hearts. Thank You for the mystery of the rebirth of the spirit of man.

It's time to go into the oil room
To make our way, we fight to stay
Down low, a bended bow.

It's here we get oil for our lamps
To feed our wicks, our hearts to fix
And burn and yearn for more of his Presence.

Run into this place of holy love and fire
We dream; will I burn? will I be seen?
Will licks and flames from me be clean?

Flap your broken wings into the oil room
To feast and fill and fuel a pool full
For this thirsty spirit,
This parched bowl, This waiting lampstand

Healing

My life is all about waiting. It seems like we're always waiting for something. Scripture is full of words inviting us to wait upon the Lord, to wait for Him to deliver, to speak, to heal, to reveal Himself.

In the midst of this long pathway out of suffering, I often recalled the moment when God supernaturally healed me from severe endometriosis. It happened on the last day in May, and I had just turned forty. I had been crying out to God for several years to deliver relief to my battered body. I had endured several surgeries that only exacerbated my symptoms. I can't count the number of times I had been anointed with oil and prayed for. At conferences, church altars, home meetings, and restaurants, friends and acquaintances had prayed in faith.

But no healing took place.

From the late 1990s through the early 2000s, my church community had been part of a spiritual renewal that spread from Toronto all over the world. It began with a small group of believers in an industrial space at the end of an airport runway. We found ourselves immersed in this exciting time in church history. Our faith felt so big in those years.

So why wasn't I getting healed now? My mind folded and unfolded, back and forth, vacillating between the concussion symptoms and the healing power I had experienced years ago.

My earlier healing happened after I heard about a night of prayer being held by a speaker who operated in the gift of healing. Like the New Testament apostles, this gift is for the church and still operates today.

I ended up attending alone and found a seat somewhere near the back. The place was full of people. When the call came for healing, I joined all the others at the front, slipping in line somewhere.

The speaker walked amongst us and prayed along the rows, but he passed me by. I remember standing there in breathtaking pain, my posture terrible as I struggled to hold myself up. My muscles tightened around me like a girdle.

After some time, the pastor of this particular church walked over and stood in front of me. He began to pray, and as he did the power of God landed on me, causing my legs to buckle.

Through tears, I composed myself and realized that I was still in pain. Standing alone, I prayed to God: "Oh Lord, make him come back and pray for me again... make him come back, make him come back..."

I saw this pastor way down at the other end of the line, but I persisted in asking.

Suddenly, he looked up and our eyes met. He started to walk towards me, passing all the others in line. My heart pounded as I anticipated an encounter with God.

"You're in a lot of pain, aren't you?" he said, standing in front of me for a second time.

I was gushing, because God heard me. He was answering me, meeting me here. I was completely overwhelmed.

However, the pastor was calm and relaxed, enjoying the moment. "The presence of the Holy Spirit is so beautiful, isn't it?"

And I hit the floor. Down there, crumpled in a big puddle of relief and joy and exhaustion, the pain instantly left my body. All the awfulness I'd been through, the surgeries, the whole mess of it, suddenly and completely flew away. Just like that. No warning, no drama.

I got up, steadied myself, and blinked in disbelief. I felt fine, pain-free for the first time in years. I couldn't believe it!

I was just about to say these words out loud when the Holy Spirit rushed in with a warning: *Watch your words.*

"I believe! I believe!" I declared instead.

I quickly drove home, exclaiming these words over and over again. Thank You, Jesus, for this joyful and miraculous story of healing!

> Now faith is the assurance (the confirmation, the title deed) of the things [we] hope for, being the proof of things [we] do not see and the conviction of their reality [faith perceiving as real fact what is not revealed to the senses]. (Hebrews 11:1)

While I've lived to see and experience many miracles of God, I'm still living with post-concussion syndrome. I have faith and look for the proof of my conviction—my own healing, as well as healing for others. Yet in this faith, I understand that some things we just have to live with.

But as I circle back to where I started this book, on the evening of day ten of my nightmare, I remember when God showed up suddenly with His winnowing fork in hand.

Day Ten Again

That evening, I was out of my mind from the shower of broken neurons and toxic sludge pinging in my head. I had just staggered downstairs from the frightening event of thinking that someone had been in the bedroom.

Having enough sense to realize that I was suffering concussion-induced panic, I sat on the edge of the couch, recoiling from the pain and anguish. I had been desperately crying out for ten days, both looking for Jesus and searching for help from outside the laws of nature.

And then, suddenly, Jesus walked into the room.

How can I describe what happened? At first, as I fought this invisible enemy, I became aware that something was being pulled away from me. It slowly lifted up off my body. It was drawn up over my shoulders like a turtleneck sweater; I felt my head dragging through to the other end.

My panic and distress began to decrease, like air slowly leaking from a bicycle tire. In a matter of seconds, my vision cleared and my mind adjusted to the new cabin pressure.

"Something's happening," I declared. "Something *is* happening. I'm in my right mind… I'm in my right mind!"

My husband urgently turned to me. "What? What's happening?"

Exaggerated blinking. Decompression. Awe. My thoughts tumbled like marbles through a peg maze, settling into their rightful places at the bottom. In this moment, I recognized Jesus for the first time since the TBI.

Just think about that for a moment; I had spent the last ten days with a deep sense of separation from God, unable to find Him amidst the bizarre symptoms and disconnection of it all. And finally, in this moment, I heard Him say, "Here I am!"

Relief washed over me. I knew there had been a change and the darkness left. I'd thought I had lost my mind, but now Jesus had brought His winnowing fan and returned me to the land of reality.

I saw Jesus. He had been right there with me the whole time.

Lying in bed, side by side with my husband that night, holding hands, all I could say through my rolling tears was "Now I see You, Jesus… now I see You."

We need to behold Him in the eclipse and not doubt what He has taught us. Such a moment will come. It felt like driving through the mountains in a fog, the peaks hidden by low-lying puffs of grey cloud. Even though they aren't seen, we know they're there. They haven't moved.

When I think back on the state of mind that seemed to overtake me in those first few days, I recognize how easy it was to see once the Lord opened my eyes. Of course He had always been there. He'd never left me.

In the coming days, I felt hope and a restoration of my spirit. The Lord had heard my prayer and delivered me, even though I wasn't healed from the injury or liberated from all my symptoms. I would still have to walk that road. But what the Lord did in that moment was show me His faithfulness to return some stability. I had not been cut off, forgotten, or discarded. He graciously gave me back a sound mind from one of the darkest personal burials I've lived through.

The months that followed are marked by my grief for the life and person I was before the injury. I've had to recognize my limitations yet trust in the Lord when I feel hindered. And I still feel a sense of loss through moments of forgetfulness and other cognitive challenges. The healing is slow, but I can abide along the journey. I must recount the things God has taught me in past seasons of learning, gathering, and sowing. I have grasped that He cannot lie, that He is faithful and will never leave me, that I am His own child and He is my Father. And He is always near.

When we walk through seemingly dark places, even the valley of death, it's easy to fall prey to the lies hissing at us, telling us that God is not near, that He has somehow disowned us. Take note: that's when you have to choose whether to believe based on fact or faith. Look with eyes of faith even if the natural facts say otherwise. Choose to lean on and believe in Christ. Learn about the kingdom of God and understand that your faith will be tried in the time of winnowing. This is an opportunity to measure your faith and galvanize you towards the truth, the very words of Christ.

The way I hear from God has changed. I don't dream anymore, like I used to. It's difficult to remember scriptures as I meditate. I can still feel heavy, sad, and joyless, but the loss is not trust in God but rather my sense of life. It's about activity, discipline, memory, strength, and doing as I please.

I must accept my life as small, at least for now. It's not that God can't use me or give me fresh vision. No. However, I accept that I have lost my previous experience of the fullness of life in Christ, when compared to my current weakness. I sometimes still find myself fighting this, still feeling beaten down. That's when I feel grief.

But what has been lost, exactly? Time? Possibility? My expectation of what should have been? Does any of that really matter in light of eternity?

Depression sometimes knocks. Sadness sits up for a moment. I lament to God.

Then a better day brings welcome amnesia from these feelings. He often draws me with His cords of love, reminding me that He is the keeper of my heart and soul. He is the only one who knows the depths to which I've been. His light illuminates my path and lights the way I am to go. I lean into Him as I read these words of Jesus:

> For whoever is bent on saving his [temporal] life [his comfort and security here] shall lose it [eternal life]; and whoever loses his life [his comfort and security here] for My sake shall find it [life everlasting]. (Matthew 16:25)

My life is not to be found here on the temporal earth. Nor is it to be found in title, name, citizenship, or talent.

So I ask myself, where do I find my life? Father, show me if there is any life other than You.

Although I have lost my life, in a sense, through it comes the experience of turning over the soil, moving the rocks and stones of offence, and pushing aside the clumps of dirt that prevent seeds from taking root.

We have to prepare the ground for fresh planting. His seeds of promise must land in cultivated soil, ready and waiting to accept them.

So He begins to plant again. Into the dark, cold ground of death, the seeds tumble. And like me, they wait. These seeds contain the promise of fruitfulness, of life in abundance here—and eternal life over there. The seeds will germinate in time, and at the right moment the new life will emerge out of the warming ground, sprouting up into the bright sunshine of day.

Here we are! Here I am, living in His promise that His Word is alive in me, this great hope we have in Christ. I am bearing good fruit because I am His and He is mine.

We find treasure when Jesus enters into our suffering. And as we oscillate between overcoming and suffering, we experience peace. Jesus said,

In the world you have tribulation and trials and distress and frustration; but be of good cheer [take courage; be confident, certain, undaunted]! For I have overcome the world. (John 16:33)

We read in Romans 8:28,

We are assured and know that [God being a partner in their labor] all things work together and are [fitting into a plan] for good to and for those who love God and are called according to [His] design and purpose.

We can be still and listen to I AM, the same One who said He is with us, that He is the resurrection, the bread of life, the door, and the way, the truth, and the life. Jesus is with you in suffering. Even when shrouded in doubt, the dark night of the soul, Christ enters our suffering and bears us up.

The threshing and winnowing is complete, for now. The chaff has been removed. What's left is good grain for making bread, for eating, for sharing. Now the grain is ground down to become bread. And like the leftover baskets after the feeding of the five thousand, we give our lives away and feed others with the food of the gospel.

He has done it. It is finished. Although I have little, let it feed crowds in His name.

Once uncovered, our faith shines like pure gold. Gold and silver are refined through fire. When heated, all the impurities are removed, leaving only the purest and cleanest metal. Fine jewellery can be crafted from what remains, as well as artwork and even building materials. When the fire comes, it drives up the value of the gold. First the threshing, then the winnowing. What remains is eternal.

As I look back on my journal, I found this entry:

Coming out of this feels like a resurrection or awakening from a coma. I feel like I've lost something precious from and in the sufferings. It's almost a grief or mourning that it's almost over. Why? Because in sufferings of all sorts, there is deep fellowship with Christ. It's a hidden place you walk alone. You dig, you search, you reach for Christ in ways we neglect, sadly, from day to day. When Christ helps us out and up, back to life again, we love Him more, leaning on our beloved, clinging to the resurrected body of Christ. We find Him here in the pain and He finds me wallowing in my weakness and fear. But He comes and lets me see Him here and causes me to pass under his counting hand. It's the Good Shepherd and His sheep.

Wow! What a comfort it is to know that we pass under the counting hand of the Good Shepherd. His watchful eye, His caring gaze, tethers me to Him.

The riches found in suffering can only be granted through the winnowing process. You can't get them from any human being or from reading and studying good books. This gold we're invited to claim can only be wrought in the fire of purification—and it is totally and completely worthwhile because its value is eternal.

But what if nothing in me changes through the fire? What if I stay the same? It's a true spiritual tragedy when a man or woman is taken through the refining fires of God yet emerges unchanged. Do we respond by trying to quickly cover up the things God is refining out of our lives? Do we harden our hearts and turn away when He brings the winnowing fan?

Could it be that we have thought our faith great for so many years when in fact it doesn't measure up? Only when we require our faith's stability to move us forward do we see the truth of that smaller measure, and only then do we notice that our faith is not what we thought.

Blow, winds of God, blow. Blow away the chaff with Your holy winnowing.

> For I consider that the sufferings of this present time (this present life) are not worth being compared with the glory that is about to be revealed to us and in us and for us and conferred on us! (Romans 8:18)

A Slow Prayer

I renew and rededicate my life to you this day,
To be filled with you
To the brim,
Overflowing with you,
Your words spilling out of me,
So only you and your words come from me—
Not needing to be pressed out any longer,
But flowing out, spoken true and right
Given out like bread,
More than enough for all.
Every fragment is life, "life bread,"
Given and broken and shared,
Renewing the poor in spirit,
Reviving the hungry and weary one,
Satisfying the childlike heart,
Served and received in love.
Bread of life, of my life,
May my little feed crowds as you multiply every
piece to every soul
True food.
Bread of life, of my life,
I dedicate myself to you anew today.

About the Author

Teena Ferrara enjoys the literary expression of creative prose, poetry, and godly inspiration while running an open mic poetry group/workshop. In the past, she was a regular contributor to *Beautiful One* magazine and hosted a weekly radio program. Teena has been involved in many leadership roles both locally and nationally, including hosting and organizing conferences, leading a national house of prayer, and hosting house groups with her husband. She has travelled to many countries, speaking at retreats, conferences, and churches. She is a wife, mother, baba, and lover of meeting the One who loves her soul in communion and prayer. You can find her kayaking, making bread, and snuggling her grandchildren.

You can reach Teena at teenaferrara@gmail.com.

Endnotes

1 Samuel Rutherford, "The Letters of Samuel Rutherford Quotes," Goodreads. Date of access: December 7, 2023 (https://www.goodreads.com/work/quotes/334769-the-letters-of-samuel-rutherford).

2 Frances R. Havergal, "Take My Life and Let It Be," 1874.

3 Charles Haddon Spurgeon, "I have learned…" Goodreads. Date of access: December 8, 2023 (https://www.goodreads.com/quotes/1199735-i-have-learned-to-kiss-the-waves-that-throw-me).

4 Catherine Doherty, Poustinia: The Desert Where the Word Speaks (Combermere, ON: Madonna House Publications, 1993), 21.

5 Henri Nouwen, The Way of the Heart (New York, NY: Ballantine Books, 1981), 17.

6 Ibid.

7 A.W. Tozer, From the Grave (Chicago, IL: Moody Publishers, 2017), 15.

8 Duncan Campbell, Revival in the Hebrides (Bolton, ON: Kraus House, 2016).

9 Included by permission of the artist.